NEW RIVER GORGE NATIONAL PARK

ACTIVITY BOOK

PUZZLES, MAZES, GAMES, AND MORE ABOUT NEW RIVER GORGE NATIONAL PARK

NATIONAL PARKS ACTIVITIES SERIES

NEW RIVER GORGE NATIONAL PARK ACTIVITY BOOK

Published by Little Bison Press

The author acknowledges that the land that is now New River Gorge National Park are the traditional lands of the Moneton, Tutelo, and S'atsoyaha (Yuchi).

LITTLE BISON Press

For more free national parks activities, visit Littlebisonpress.com

About New River Gorge National Park

New River Gorge National Park is located in the US state of West Virginia. The park's namesake river is one of the oldest rivers on the continent. It flows through the Appalachian Mountain Range.

This park is famous for all of the activities you can do on the river. Between kayaking and rafting, fishing, and swimming, this park has activities for everyone. You can enjoy fun things on the New River, but take care as you do. The river has swift currents, deep holes, and a rocky bottom. Learn about river safety before you participate in water-related activities.

Visitors from all over the world come to this area to go rock climbing. There are over 1400 rock climbing routes for people to attempt. The sandstone cliffs in the area have lots of features, which are bumps or indentations in the rock where climbers put their hands and feet to move up the rock face.

New River Gorge National Park is famous for:

- historic remnants of the lumber and coal industries
- water activities
- rock climbing

Hey! I'm Parker!

I'm the only snail in history to visit every national park in the United States! Come join me on my adventures in New River Gorge National Park.

Throughout this book, we will learn about the history of the park, the animals and plants that live here, and things to do here if you ever get to visit in person. This book is also full of games and activities!

Last but not least, I am hidden 9 times on different pages. See how many times you can find me. This page doesn't count!

West Virginia Bingo

Let's play bingo! Cross off each box that you are able to during your visit to the national park. Try to get a bingo down, across, or diagonally. If you can't visit the park, use the bingo board to plan your perfect trip.

Pick out some activities that you would want to do during your visit. What would you do first? How long would you spend there? What animals would you try to see?

SPOT A SOMEONE BASE JUMPING	WADE IN THE RIVER	IDENTIFY A TREE	TAKE A PICTURE AT AN OVERLOOK	WATCH A MOVIE AT THE VISITORS CENTER
GO FOR A HIKE	LEARN ABOUT THE INDIGENOUS PEOPLE THAT LIVE IN THIS AREA	WITNESS A SUNRISE OR SUNSET	OBSERVE THE NIGHT SKIES	GO ROCK CLIMBING
HEAR A BIRD CALL	LEARN ABOUT THE COAL MINING HISTORY	 FREE SPACE	GO FLY FISHING	VISIT A RANGER STATION
PICK UP TEN PIECES OF TRASH	GO CAMPING	SEE A PEREGRINE FALCON	VISIT THURMOND, WEST VIRGINIA	SPOT A BIRD OF PREY
LEARN ABOUT THE GEOLOGY OF THE RIVER	GO WHITE WATER RAFTING	HAVE A PICNIC	SPOT SOME ANIMAL TRACKS	PARTICIPATE IN A RANGER-LED ACTIVITY

The National Park Logo

The National Park System has over 400 units in the US. Just like New River Gorge National Park, each location is unique or special in some way. The areas include other national parks, historic sites, monuments, seashores, and other recreation areas.

Each element of the National Park emblem represents something that the National Park Service protects. Fill in each blank below to show what each symbol represents.

WORD BANK:
MOUNTAINS, ARROWHEAD, BISON, SEQUOIA TREE, WATER

This represents all plants. ____________________

This represents all animals. ____________________

This symbol represents the landscapes. ____________________

This represents the waters protected by the park service. ____________________

This represents the historical and archeological values. ____________________

Now it's your turn! Pretend you are designing a new national park. Add elements to the design that represent the things that your park protects

What is the name of your park?

Describe why you included the symbols that you included. What do they mean?

Things to Do Jumble

Unscramble the letters to uncover activities you can do while in New River Gorge National Park. Hint: each one ends in -ing.

1. BOTA
☐☐☐☐ING

2. KHI
☐☐☐ING

3. IRDB
☐☐☐☐ING

4. MACP
☐☐☐☐ING

5. KINICPC
☐☐☐☐☐☐☐ING

6. EISSTEHG
☐☐☐☐☐☐☐☐ING

7. SHOSEWON
☐☐☐☐☐☐☐ING

Word Bank

- birding
- reading
- camping
- snowshoeing
- boating
- hiking
- hunting
- singing
- yelling
- sightseeing
- picnicking

Weather Watch

Find a place where you are in an open area where you can easily see the sky. Complete the activities below to provide your weather report. If you aren't in the park, you can do this activity from home.

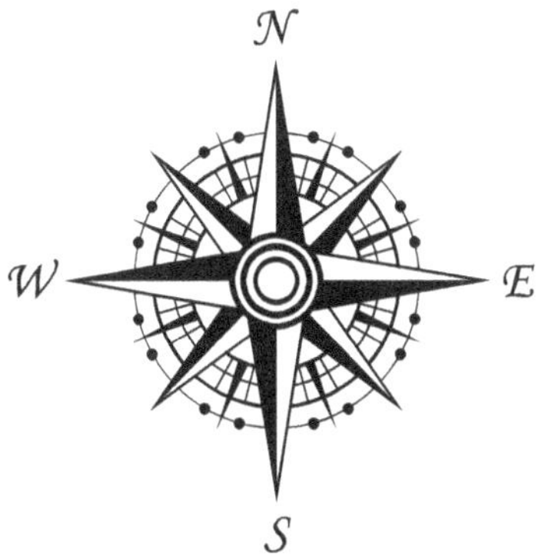

Can you feel any wind?

What does the sky look like?

Is there anything you notice about the weather today?

What is the date?

What is the time?

Where is the sun in the sky? (rising, midpoint, falling)

What direction is the wind blowing?

Are there clouds in the sky? If so, draw them below:

Go Birdwatching on the Kaymoor Miner's Trail

start
here

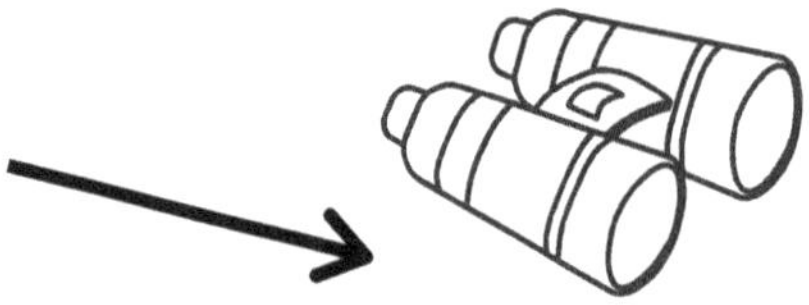

DID YOU KNOW?
New River Gorge National Park is home to several birds of prey, including eagles, falcons, and owls. Birds of prey are birds that hunt other animals for food.

Camping Packing List

What should you take with you camping? Pretend you are in charge of your family camping trip. Make a list of what you would need to be safe and comfortable on an overnight excursion. Some considerations are listed on the side.

1.
2.
3.
4.
5.
6.
7.
8.
9.
10.
11.
12.
13.
14.
15.
16.

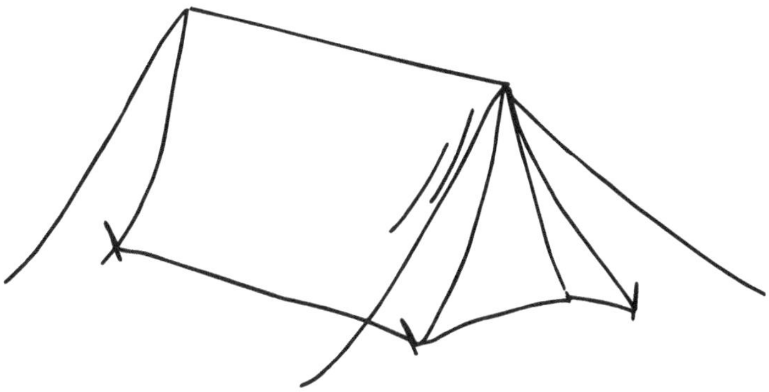

- What will you eat at every meal?
- What will the weather be like?
- Where will you sleep?
- What will you do during your free time?
- How luxurious do you want camp to be?
- How will you cook?
- How will you see at night?
- How will you dispose of trash?
- What might you need in case of emergencies?

New River Gorge National Park

Visitor's Log

Date:

Season:

Who I went with:

Which entrance:

How was your experience? Write a few sentences on your trip. Where did you stay? What did you do? What was your favorite activity? If you have not yet visited the park, write a paragraph pretending that you did.

STAMPS

Many national parks and monuments have cancellation stamps for visitors to use. These rubber stamps record the date and the location that you visited. Many people collect the markings as a free souvenir. Check with a ranger to see where you can find a stamp during your visit. If you aren't able to find one, you can draw your own.

Where is the Park?

New River Gorge National Park is in the eastern United States. It is located in West Virginia. West Virginia borders the states of Pennsylvania, Ohio, Maryland, Virginia, and Kentucky.

West Virginia

Look at the shape of West Virgina. Can you find it on the map? If you are from the US, can you find your home state? Color West Virginia red. Put a star on the map where you live.

Color The Bridge

The New River Gorge Bridge is a steel arch bridge over the New River Gorge near Fayetteville, West Virginia. With an arch 1,700 feet (518 m) long, the New River Gorge Bridge was once the world's longest single-span bridge. Now it is the fifth-longest.

The Eastern Garter Snake is very common in New River Gorge National Park. Some people mispronounce their names as "garden snakes" because they are often seen in home gardens.

Black bears live in the park. If you are lucky enough to see one, remember to never approach it.

Who lives here?

Here are eight plants and animals that live in the park.
Use the word bank to fill in the clues below.

WORD BANK: GARTER SNAKE, HAWK, PEREGRINE, HELLBENDER, INDIANA BAT, GROUNDHOG, BLACK BEAR, BEAVER

□□□□N□□□□

□□□□□■□E□□

□□W□

□□□□□R□□□

□□□I□□□■□□□

□□□V□□

□□□□□E□□□□

□□□□□R■□□□□□

Peregrines are known for being the fastest birds in the world. They can reach speeds of 200 miles per hour when hunting.

Beavers are the largest North American rodent.

Common Names
vs.
Scientific Names

A common name of an organism is a name that is based on everyday language. You have heard the common names of plants, animals, and other living things on tv, in books, and at school. Common names can also be referred to as "English" names, popular names, or farmer's name. Common names can vary from place to place. The word for a particular tree may be one thing, but that same tree has a different name in another country. Common names can even vary from region to region, even in the same country.

Scientific names, or Latin names, are given to organisms to make it possible to have uniform names for the same species. Scientific names are in Latin. You may have heard plants or animals referred to by their scientific name, or at least parts of their scientific names. Latin names are also called "binomial nomenclature" which refers to a two-part naming system. The first part of the name - the generic name –names the genus to which the species belongs. The second part of the name, the specific name, identifies the species. For example, Tyrannosaurus rex is an example of a widely known scientific name.

American Black Bear

Ursus americanus

COMMON NAME

North American Beaver

Castor canadensis

LATIN NAME = GENUS + SPECIES

American Black Bear = Ursus americanus

North American Beaver = Castor canadensis

Find the Match!
Common Names and Latin Names

Match the common name to the scientific name for each animal. The first one is done for you. Use clues on the page before and after this one to complete the matches.

North American Beaver	Haliaeetus leucocephalus
Big Rhododendron	Ursus americanus
White Oak	Crytobranchus alleganiensis
American Black Bear	Falco peregrinus
Great Horned Owl	Rhododendron maximum
Bald Eagle	Thamnophis sirtalis sirtalis
Hellbender	Bubo virginianus
Peregrine Falcon	Castor canadensis
Eastern Garter Snake	Quercus alba

Bald Eagle

Haliaeetus leucocephalus

Peregrine Falcon
Falco peregrinus

Bald Eagle
Haliaeetus leucocephalus

Great Horned Owl
Bubo virginianus

Some plants and animals that live at the New River Gorge

White Oak
Quercus alba

Big Rhododendron
Rhododendron maximum

Eastern Garter Snake
Thamnophis sirtalis sirtalis

Take a Hike

Go for a hike with your friends or family. If you aren't able to visit New River Gorge National Park, go for a walk in a park near where you live. Read through the prompts before your walk and finish the activities after you return.

Draw something you saw that moves:

Draw something you saw when you looked up:

Draw something you saw that grows out of the ground:

Draw a picture of your favorite part of the walk:

The Ten Essentials

The ten essentials is a list of things that are important to have when you go for longer hikes. If you go on a hike to the <u>backcountry</u>, it is especially important that you have everything you need in case of an emergency. If you get lost or something unforeseen happens, it is good to be prepared to survive until help finds you.

The ten essentials list was developed in the 1930s by an outdoors group called the Mountaineers. Over time and technological advancements, this list has evolved. Can you identify all the things on the current list? Circle each of the "essentials" and cross out everything that doesn't make the cut.

fire: matches, lighter, tinder and/or stove	a pint of milk	extra money	headlamp plus extra batteries	extra clothes
extra water	a dog	Polaroid camera	bug net	lightweight games, like a deck of cards
extra food	a roll of duct tape 	shelter	sun protection like sunglasses, sun-protective clothes and sunscreen	knife: plus a gear repair kit
a mirror	navigation: map, compass, altimeter, GPS device, or satellite messenger	first aid kit	extra flip-flops	entertainment like video games or books

Backcountry- a remote undeveloped rural area.

Protecting the Park

When you visit national parks, it is important to leave the park the way you found it. Did you know that the national parks get hundreds of millions of visitors every year? We can only protect national parks for future visitors to enjoy if everyone does their part. The choices that each visitor makes when visiting the park have a big impact all together.

Read each line below. Write a sentence or draw a picture to show the impacts these changes would make on the park.

What would happen if every visitor fed the wild animals?

What would happen if every visitor picked a flower?

What would happen if every visitor took home a few rocks?

What would happen if every visitor wrote or carved their name on the rocks or trees?

Connect the Dots

Connect the dots to figure out what this tiny critter is. This critter is one of many other species of birds that live in New River Gorge National Park.

Their heart rate can reach as high as 1,260 beats per minute and a breathing rate of 250 breaths per minute. Have you ever measured your breathing rate? Ask a friend or family member to set a timer for 60 seconds. Once they say "go", try to breathe normally. Count each breath until they say "stop." How do your breaths per minute compare to hummingbirds?

LISTEN CAREFULLY

Visitors to New River Gorge National Park may hear different noises from those they hear at home. Try this activity to experience this for yourself!

First, find a place outside where it is comfortable to sit or stand for a few minutes. You can do this by yourself or with a friend or family member. Once you have a good spot, close your eyes and listen. Be quiet for one minute and pay attention to what you are hearing. List some of the sounds you have heard in one of the two boxes below:

NATURAL SOUNDS
MADE BY ANIMALS, TREES OR PLANTS, THE WIND, ETC

HUMAN-MADE SOUNDS
MADE BY PEOPLE, MACHINES, ETC

ONCE YOU ARE BACK AT HOME, TRY REPEATING YOUR EXPERIMENT:

NATURAL SOUNDS
MADE BY ANIMALS, TREES OR PLANTS, THE WIND, ETC

HUMAN-MADE SOUNDS
MADE BY PEOPLE, MACHINES, ETC

WHERE DID YOU HEAR MORE NATURAL SOUNDS? ____________________

WHERE DID YOU HEAR MORE HUMAN SOUNDS? ____________________

Draw A Meal

Imagine you've been adventuring all day and now it's time to go back to camp for the night. You are hungry!

Draw the meal that you will cook over the campfire.

New River Gorge Word Search

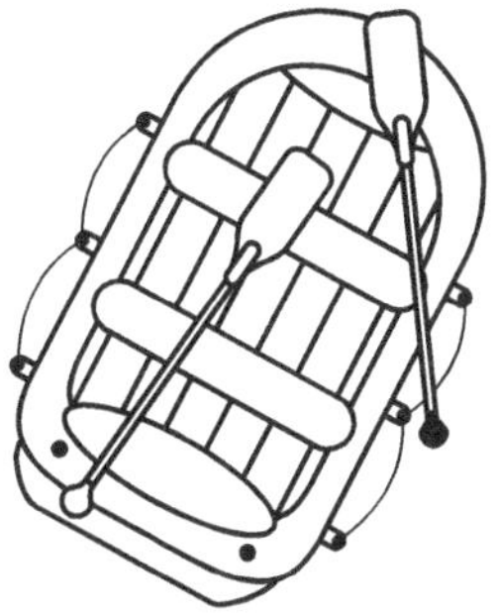

Words may be horizontal, vertical, or diagonal and they might be backward!

1. West Virginia
2. river
3. rafting
4. wildflowers
5. whitewater
6. coal
7. peregrine
8. fishing
9. climbing
10. Thurmond
11. railroad
12. deer
13. bridge
14. Grandview
15. Sandstone Falls
16. Endless Wall
17. bat
18. woodrat

S	M	R	E	W	I	L	D	F	L	O	W	E	R	S
R	A	F	T	I	N	G	T	O	R	B	R	N	A	W
I	W	N	O	E	P	C	L	I	M	B	I	N	G	H
V	C	H	D	E	E	R	C	L	T	C	B	U	H	I
E	A	F	A	S	E	S	T	E	S	A	P	W	A	T
R	J	I	S	L	T	H	U	R	M	O	N	D	I	E
P	O	S	O	V	E	O	S	B	H	T	A	S	N	W
E	L	H	A	G	R	A	N	D	V	I	E	W	I	A
R	T	I	T	M	D	L	A	E	R	E	L	W	G	T
E	S	N	U	L	E	E	R	T	F	N	A	O	R	E
G	G	G	R	F	W	O	O	D	R	A	T	S	I	R
R	N	B	A	T	F	R	G	R	K	H	L	A	V	A
I	I	E	I	I	A	I	O	I	C	O	A	L	T	N
N	P	B	L	R	S	C	N	N	A	M	C	N	S	P
E	M	N	R	E	R	I	D	B	R	I	D	G	E	O
I	K	A	O	A	K	I	N	G	E	R	A	Q	W	N
O	C	R	A	G	D	E	E	O	O	O	R	V	W	D
N	E	N	D	L	E	S	S	W	A	L	L	A	D	M

Find the Match!

What are Baby Animals Called?

Match the animal to its baby. The first one is done for you.

Elk	eaglet
Bald Eagle	calf
Little Brown Bat	snakelets
Striped Skunk	pup
Great Horned Owl	owlet
Western Toad	kit
Mountain Lion	tadpole
Garter snake	kitten

Bird Scavenger Hunt

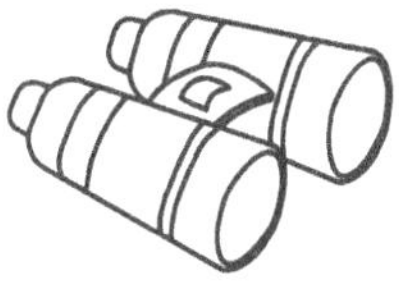

New River Gorge National Park is a great place to go birdwatching. You don't have to be able to identify different species of birds in order to have fun. Open your eyes and tune in your ears. Check off as many birds on this list as you can.

- [ ] A colorful bird
- [ ] A brown bird
- [ ] A bird in a tree
- [ ] A bird with long tail feathers
- [ ] A bird making noise
- [ ] A bird eating or hunting
- [ ] A bird with spots
- [ ] A big bird
- [ ] A small bird
- [ ] A hopping bird
- [ ] A flying bird
- [ ] A bird's nest
- [ ] A bird's footprint on the ground
- [ ] A bird with stripes somewhere on it

What was the easiest bird on the list to find? What was the hardest? Why do you think that was?

___

___

___

The Perfect Picnic Spot

Fill in the blanks on this page without looking at the full story. Once you have each line filled out, use the words you've chosen to complete the story on the next page.

EMOTION_______________________________________

FOOD_______________________________________

SOMETHING SWEET_______________________________________

STORE_______________________________________

MODE OF TRANSPORTATION_______________________________________

NOUN_______________________________________

SOMETHING ALIVE_______________________________________

SAUCE_______________________________________

PLURAL VEGETABLES_______________________________________

ADJECTIVE_______________________________________

PLURAL BODY PART_______________________________________

ANIMAL_______________________________________

PLURAL FRUIT_______________________________________

PLACE_______________________________________

SOMETHING TALL_______________________________________

COLOR_______________________________________

ADJECTIVE_______________________________________

NOUN_______________________________________

A DIFFERENT ANIMAL_______________________________________

FAMILY MEMBER #1 _______________________________________

FAMILY MEMBER #2 _______________________________________

VERB THAT ENDS IN -ING _______________________________________

A DIFFERENT FOOD_______________________________________

The Perfect Picnic Spot

Use the words from the previous page to complete a silly story.

When my family suggested having our lunch at the Cathedral Falls picnic area,

I was ________. I love eating my ______ outside! I knew we had picked up a
EMOTION FOOD

box of ______ from the _________ for after lunch, my favorite. We drove up
SOMETHING SWEET STORE

to the area and I jumped out of the _________. "I will find the perfect spot for
MODE OF TRANSPORTATION

a picnic!" I grabbed a ______ for us to sit on, and I ran off. I passed a picnic
NOUN

table, but it was covered with ________ so we couldn't sit there. The next
SOMETHING ALIVE

picnic table looked okay, but there were smears of _______ and pieces of
SAUCE

________ everywhere. The people that were there before must have been
PLURAL VEGETABLES

______! I gritted my _______ together and kept walking down the path,
ADJECTIVE PLURAL BODY PART

determined to find the perfect spot. I wanted a table with a good view of the

falls. Why was this so hard? If we were lucky, I might even get to see ______
ANIMAL

eating some ______ on the cliffside. They don't have those in _______ where I
PLURAL FRUIT PLACE

am from. I walked down a little hill and there it was, the perfect spot! The trees

towered overhead and looked as tall as ________. The patch of grass was a
SOMETHING TALL

beautiful _______ color. The ______ flowers were growing on
COLOR ADJECTIVE

the side of a _______. I looked across the water's edge and even saw a
NOUN

_________ on the edge of a rock. I looked back to see my __________ and
DIFFERENT ANIMAL FAMILY MEMBER #1

__________ _________ a picnic basket. "I hope you brought plenty of
FAMILY MEMBER #2 VERB THAT ENDS IN ING

________, I'm starving!"
A DIFFERENT FOOD

Hike to a Waterfall

start
here

DID YOU KNOW?
You can visit many different waterfalls at New River Gorge National Park.

Rockclimbing Route Names

A climbing route is a specific path for climbing up a rock wall. Different features provide handholds and footholds to get climbers to the top. Rock climbers have a reputation for naming their routes quirky names. Find these route names in the word search below.

1. Barb Wire
2. Burning Calves
3. Chewy
4. Chuckles
5. Fantasy
6. Fishbone
7. Floaters
8. Jaws
9. New Yosemite
10. Ritz Cracker
11. Smore Energy
12. Spiderwalk
13. Super Crack
14. Supermoon
15. Werewolf
16. Wild seed
17. Zag
18. Barfing Butterflies

B	B	N	E	W	Y	O	S	E	M	I	T	E	R	S
Z	A	G	T	I	C	H	U	C	K	L	E	S	A	W
I	R	R	O	E	P	C	P	I	M	B	I	P	G	H
V	F	F	L	O	A	T	E	R	S	C	B	I	H	I
E	I	B	A	I	E	S	R	E	S	A	P	D	A	T
R	N	I	U	L	N	H	M	R	J	C	H	E	W	Y
P	G	S	O	R	E	G	O	B	H	T	A	R	N	W
W	B	H	A	G	N	A	O	D	V	J	A	W	S	A
I	U	R	N	M	D	I	N	F	A	N	T	A	S	Y
L	T	N	U	L	E	E	N	T	T	N	A	L	R	F
D	T	G	R	F	W	O	O	G	R	T	T	K	I	I
S	E	B	A	S	U	P	E	R	C	R	A	C	K	S
E	R	I	W	B	R	A	B	I	C	A	A	R	T	H
E	F	I	S	H	B	O	N	E	A	M	L	N	S	P
D	L	N	R	E	R	I	D	B	R	I	D	V	E	O
R	I	T	Z	C	R	A	C	K	E	R	A	Q	E	N
O	E	R	A	G	D	F	L	O	W	E	R	E	W	S
N	S	M	O	R	E	E	N	E	R	G	Y	A	D	M

? If you were to name a route, what would you call it? Ask a family member or friend the same question.

Leave No Trace Quiz

Leave No Trace is a concept that helps people make decisions during outdoor recreation that protects the environment. There are seven principles that guide us when we spend time outdoors, whether you are in a national park or not. Are you an expert in Leave No Trace? Take this quiz and find out!

1. How can you plan ahead and prepare to ensure you have the best experience you can in the national park?
   a. Make sure you stop by the ranger station for a map and to ask about current conditions.
   b. Just wing it! You will know the best trail when you see it.
   c. Stick to your plan, even if conditions change. You traveled a long way to get here, and you should stick to your plan.
2. What is an example of traveling on a durable surface?
   a. Walking only on the designated path.
   b. Walking on the grass that borders the trail if the trail is very muddy.
   c. Taking a shortcut if you can find one since it means you will be walking less.
3. Why should you dispose of waste properly?
   a. You don't need to. Park rangers love to pick up the trash you leave behind.
   b. You actually should leave your leftovers behind, because animals will eat them. It is important to make sure they aren't hungry.
   c. So that other peoples' experiences of the park are not impacted by you leaving your waste behind.
4. How can you best follow the concept "leave what you find"?
   a. Take only a small rock or leaf to remember your trip.
   b. Take pictures, but leave any physical items where they are.
   c. Leave everything you find, unless it may be rare like an arrowhead, then it is okay to take.
5. What is not a good example of minimizing campfire impacts?
   a. Only having a campfire in a pre-existing campfire ring.
   b. Checking in with current conditions when you consider making a campfire.
   c. Building a new campfire ring in a location that has a better view.
6. What is a poor example of respecting wildlife?
   a. Building squirrel houses out of rocks so the squirrels have a place to live.
   b. Stay far away from wildlife and give them plenty of space.
   c. Reminding your grown-ups to not drive too fast in animal habitats while visiting the park.
7. How can you show consideration of other visitors?
   a. Play music on your speaker so other people at the campground can enjoy it.
   b. Wear headphones on the trail if you choose to listen to music.
   c. Make sure to yell "Hello!" to every animal you see at top volume.

Park Poetry

America's parks inspire art of all kinds. Painters, sculptors, photographers, writers, and artists of all mediums have taken inspiration from natural beauty. They have turned their inspiration into great works.

Use this space to write your own poem about the park. Think about what you have experienced or seen. Use descriptive language to create an acrostic poem. This type of poem has the first letter of each line spell out another word. Create an acrostic that spells out the word "Gorge."

G ______________________________

O ______________________________

R ______________________________

G ______________________________

E ______________________________

Great views
Orange flowers growing
Reaching toward the sky
Golden moments
E scape into nature

Glowing sky
Overhead, a bird
Rushes through the sky
Going home for the night
E vening settles

Exploring the Dark Sky

This park is a popular destination for stargazing. You may see stars in the night sky here that you may not see at home. Why do you think that is?

For all of time, people from across the world have looked at the night sky and seen images in the stars. They created stories about groups of stars, also called constellations. Create your own constellation that you see in the starfield below!

Catch a Fish in the New River

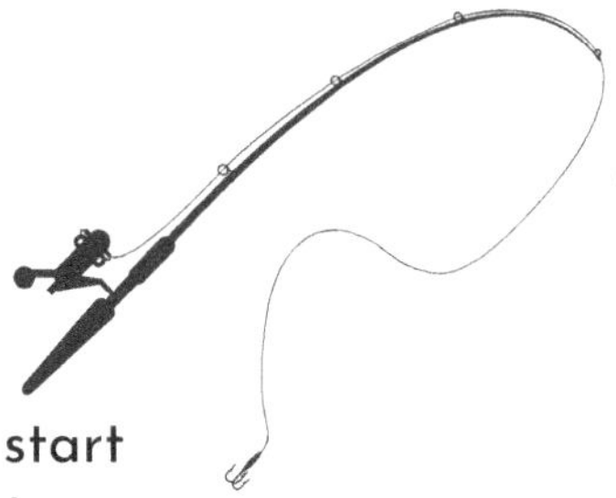

start here

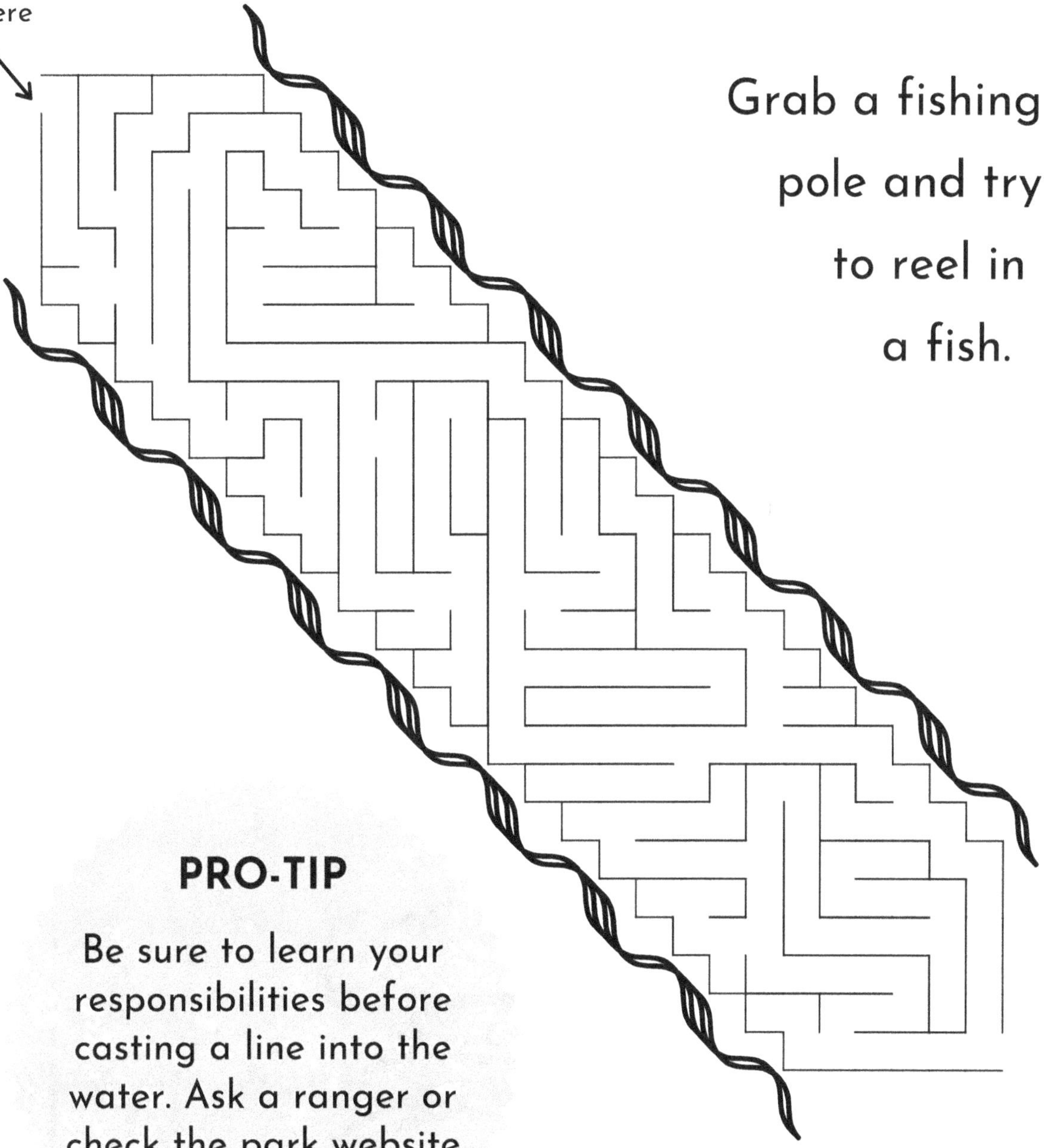

Grab a fishing pole and try to reel in a fish.

PRO-TIP

Be sure to learn your responsibilities before casting a line into the water. Ask a ranger or check the park website before you go.

Stacking Rocks

Have you ever seen stacks of rocks while hiking in national parks? Do you know what they are or what they mean? These rock piles are called cairns and often mark hiking routes in parks. Every park has a different way to maintain trails and cairns. However, they all have the same rule: If you come across a cairn, do not disturb it.

Color the cairn and the rules to remember.

1. Do not tamper with cairns.

If a cairn is tampered with or an unauthorized one is built, then future visitors may become disoriented or even lost.

2. Do not build unauthorized cairns.

Moving rocks disturbs the soil and makes the area more prone to erosion. Disturbing rocks can disturb fragile plants.

3. Do not add to existing cairns.

Authorized cairns are carefully designed. Adding to them can actually cause them to collapse.

Decoding Using American Sign Language

American Sign Language, also called ASL for short, is a language that many people who are deaf or hard of hearing use to communicate. People use ASL to communicate with their hands. Did you know people from all over the country and world travel to national parks? You may hear people speaking other languages. You might also see people using ASL. Use the American Manual Alphabet chart to decode some national parks facts.

This was the first national park to be established:

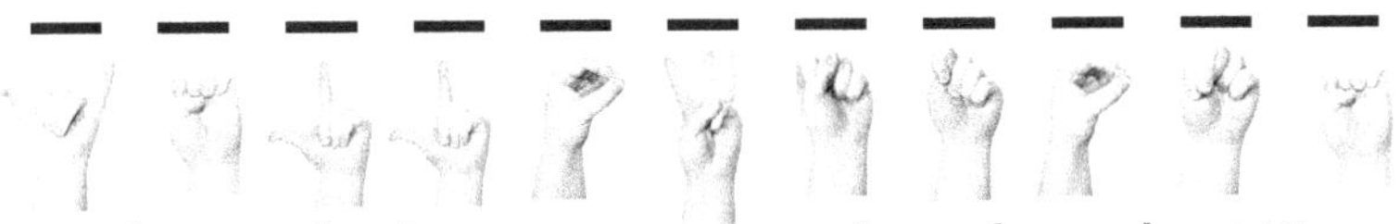

This is the biggest national park in the US:

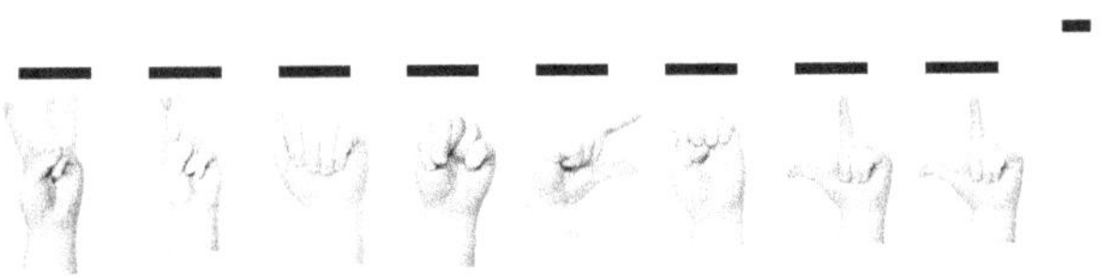

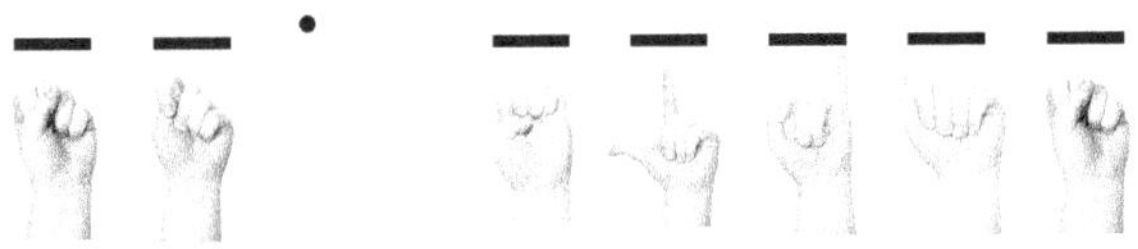

This is the most visited national park:

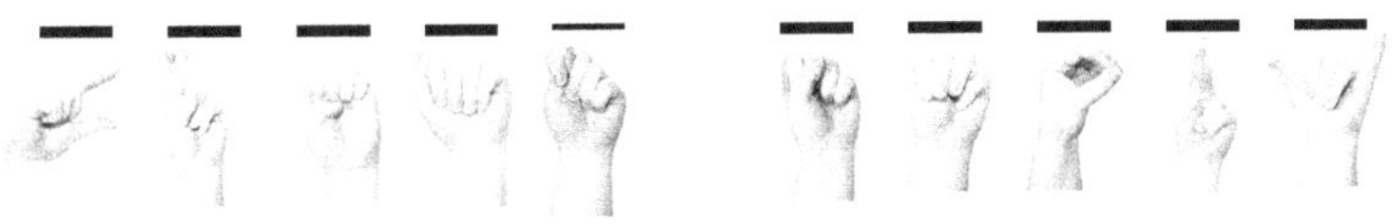

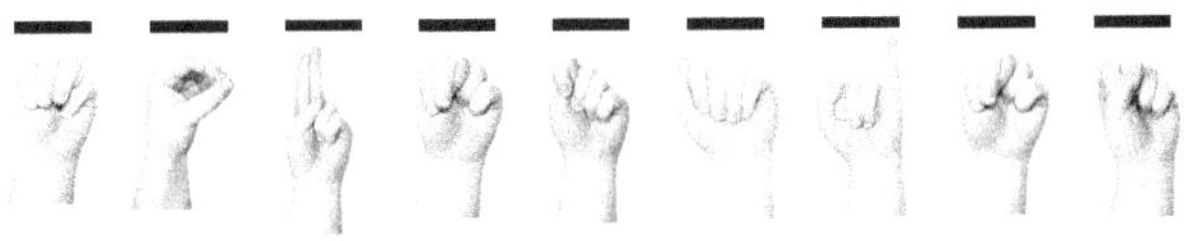

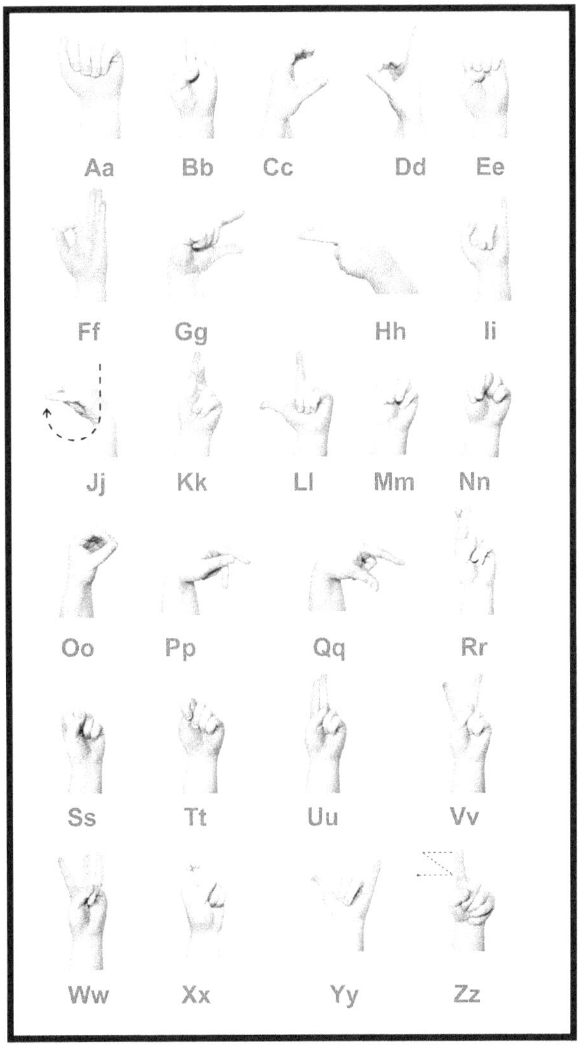

Hint: Pay close attention to the position of the thumb!

Try it! Using the chart, try to make the letters of the alphabet with your hand. What is the hardest letter to make? Can you spell out your name? Show a friend or family member and have them watch you spell out the name of the national park you are in.

Go Bicycling on the Arrowhead Trails

DID YOU KNOW?

Mountain Biking is a popular activity in New River Gorge National Park National Park.

start here

Don't forget to wear a helmet!

Butterflies of the West Virginia

Many species of butterflies and moths live in New River Gorge National Park. Their wingspan size varies, as do the patterns on their wings. Design your own butterfly below. Make sure the wings are symmetrical, meaning both sides match.

A Hike at Grandview

Fill in the blanks on this page without looking at the full story. Once you have each line filled out, use the words you've chosen to complete the story on the next page.

ADJECTIVE ______________________________

SOMETHING TO EAT ______________________________

SOMETHING TO DRINK ______________________________

NOUN ______________________________

ARTICLE OF CLOTHING ______________________________

BODY PART ______________________________

VERB ______________________________

ANIMAL ______________________________

SAME TYPE OF FOOD ______________________________

ADJECTIVE ______________________________

SAME ANIMAL ______________________________

VERB THAT ENDS IN "ED" ______________________________

NUMBER ______________________________

A DIFFERENT NUMBER ______________________________

SOMETHING THAT FLIES ______________________________

LIGHT SOURCE ______________________________

PLURAL NOUN ______________________________

FAMILY MEMBER ______________________________

YOUR NICKNAME ______________________________

A Hike at Grandview

Use the words from the previous page to complete a silly story.

I went for a hike at Grandview today. In my favorite _______ (ADJECTIVE) backpack, I made sure to pack a map so I wouldn't get lost. I also threw in an extra ___________ (SOMETHING TO EAT) just in case I got hungry and a bottle of ___________ (SOMETHING TO DRINK). I put on my __________ (NOUN) spray, and a tied a _____________ (ARTICLE OF CLOTHING) around my __________ (BODY PART), in case it gets chilly. I started to ______ (VERB) down the path. As soon as I turned the corner, I came face to face with a(n) ________ (ANIMAL). I think it was as startled as I was! What should I do? I had to think fast! Should I give it some of my ___________ (SAME TYPE OF FOOD)? No. I had to remember what the _______ (ADJECTIVE) ranger told me. "If you see one, back away slowly and try not to scare it." Soon enough, the __________ (SAME ANIMAL) __________ (VERB THAT ENDS IN ED) away. The coast was clear. ______ (NUMBER) hours later, I finally got to the lookout. I felt like I could see for a ______ (A DIFFERENT NUMBER) miles. I took a picture of a ________ (NOUN) so I could always remember this moment. As I was putting my camera away, a _________ (SOMETHING THAT FLIES) flew by, reminding me that it was almost nighttime. I turned on my __________ (LIGHT SOURCE) and headed back. I could hear the ___________ (PLURAL INSECT) singing their evening song. Just as I was getting tired, I saw my __________ (FAMILY MEMBER) and our tent.

"Welcome back ________ (NICKNAME)! How was your hike?"

Sound Exploration

Spend a minute or two listening to all of the sounds around you.
Draw your favorite sound.

How did this sound make you feel?

____

____

What did you think when you heard this sound?

____

____

Let's Go Camping Word Search

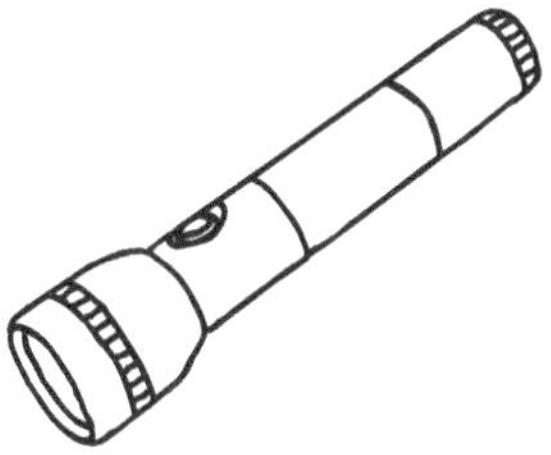

Words may be horizontal, vertical, or diagonal and they might be backward!

1. tent
2. camp stove
3. sleeping bag
4. bug spray
5. sunscreen
6. map
7. flashlight
8. pillow
9. lantern
10. ice
11. snacks
12. smores
13. water
14. first aid kit
15. chair
16. cards
17. books
18. games
19. trail
20. hat

D	P	P	I	L	L	O	W	D	B	T	E	A	C	I
E	O	A	D	P	R	E	A	A	M	B	R	C	A	N
P	W	C	A	M	P	S	T	O	V	E	I	H	X	G
R	A	H	S	G	E	L	E	B	E	E	D	A	P	S
E	L	B	U	G	S	P	R	A	Y	N	G	I	E	A
S	I	A	H	G	C	I	C	N	N	M	E	R	C	N
C	W	N	L	A	F	I	R	S	K	O	O	B	F	K
M	T	A	E	M	I	L	E	L	H	M	R	W	L	J
T	A	P	R	E	A	O	R	E	S	L	B	A	A	B
S	M	P	A	S	R	R	T	E	N	T	L	U	S	C
C	E	A	I	I	R	C	G	P	E	I	U	J	H	A
S	S	N	A	C	K	S	S	I	M	O	K	I	L	R
I	J	R	S	F	O	I	S	N	J	R	A	Q	I	D
C	Y	E	T	L	E	V	E	G	U	O	R	V	G	S
E	W	T	A	K	C	A	B	B	S	S	O	H	H	M
X	J	N	F	I	R	S	T	A	I	D	K	I	T	T
U	A	A	E	S	S	E	N	G	E	T	P	V	A	B
C	J	L	I	A	R	T	D	N	A	M	A	H	A	S

All in the Day of a Park Ranger

Park Rangers are hardworking individuals dedicated to protecting our parks, monuments, museums, and more. They take care of the natural and cultural resources for future generations. Rangers also help protect the visitors of the park. Their responsibilities are broad and they work both with the public and behind the scenes.

What have you seen park rangers do? Use your knowledge of the duties of park rangers to fill out a typical daily schedule, one activity for each hour. Feel free to make up your own, but some examples of activities are provided on the right. Read carefully, not all of the example activities are befitting a ranger!

6 am	Lead a sunrise hike
7 am	
8 am	
9 am	
10 am	
11 am	
12 pm	Enjoy a lunch break outside
1 pm	
2 pm	
3 pm	
4 pm	Teach visitors about the geology of the gorge
5 pm	
6 pm	
7 pm	
8 pm	
9 pm	

- feed the bald eagles
- build trails for visitors to enjoy
- throw rocks off the side of the mountain
- rescue lost hikers
- study animal behavior
- record air quality data
- answer questions at the visitor center
- pick wildflowers
- pick up litter
- share marshmallows with squirrels
- repair handrails
- lead a class on a field trip
- catch frogs and make them race
- lead people on educational hikes
- write articles for the park website
- protect the river from pollution
- remove non-native plants from the park
- study how climate change is affecting the park
- give a talk about mountain lions
- lead a program for campers on salmon

If you were a park ranger, which of the above tasks would you enjoy most?

____

____

Draw Yourself as a Park Ranger

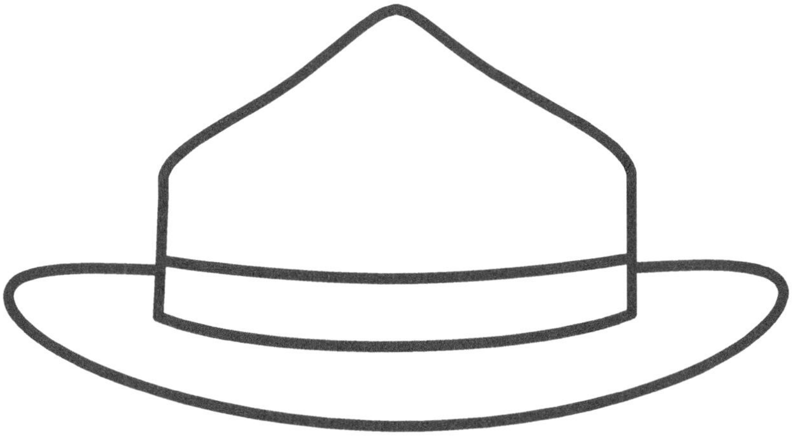

Fish of the New River

1.

2.

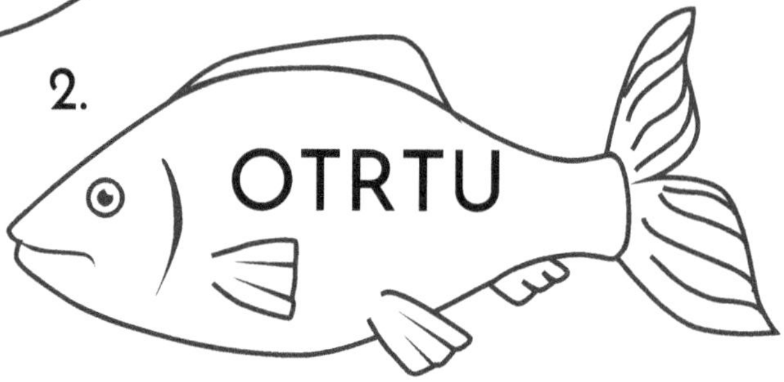

Unscramble these common fish names that live in the park.

3.

4.

5.

1. ____________________
2. ____________________
3. ____________________
4. ____________________
5. ____________________

Word Bank

bluegill
trout
carp
minnow
crappie
bass
walleye
catfish

Amphibians

Multiple species of toads and frogs live in New River Gorge National Park. West Virginia has more types of salamanders than any other state. Frogs and toads both spend the beginning of their lives the same way, as tadpoles. Tadpoles hatch from eggs in water, usually in springs or pools of water.

Both frogs and toads are amphibians. Salamanders are amphibians too. Color the salamanders below.

Photobook

Draw some pictures of things you saw in the park.

Snail Mail

Design a postcard to send to a friend or a family member. Who do you want to tell about New River Gorge National Park? In the first template, write your message. In the second template, create a design for the front of the postcard. You could show something you saw, something you did, or something you want to do in the national park.

Postcard

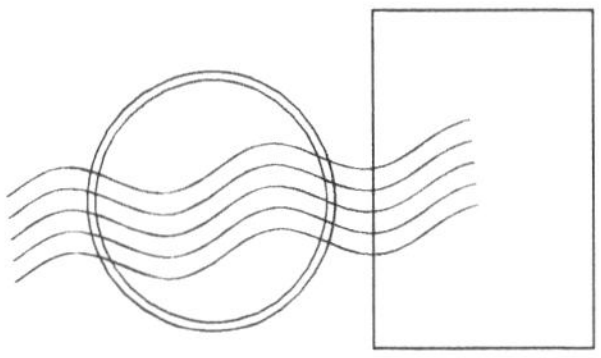

63 National Parks

How many other national parks have you been to? Which one do you want to visit next? Note that some of these parks fall on the border of more than one state, you may check it off more than once!

Alaska

☐ Denali National Park
☐ Gates of the Arctic National Park
☐ Glacier Bay National Park
☐ Katmai National Park
☐ Kenai Fjords National Park
☐ Kobuk Valley National Park
☐ Lake Clark National Park
☐ Wrangell-St. Elias National Park

American Samoa

☐ National Park of American Samoa

Arizona

☐ Grand Canyon National Park
☐ Petrified Forest National Park
☐ Saguaro National Park

Arkansas

☐ Hot Springs National Park

California

☐ Channel Islands National Park
☐ Death Valley National Park
☐ Joshua Tree National Park
☐ Kings Canyon National Park
☐ Lassen Volcanic National Park
☐ Pinnacles National Park
☐ Redwood National Park
☐ Sequoia National Park
☐ Yosemite National Park

Colorado

☐ Black Canyon of the Gunnison National Park
☐ Great Sand Dunes National Park
☐ Mesa Verde National Park
☐ Rocky Mountain National Park

Florida

☐ Biscayne National Park
☐ Dry Tortugas National Park
☐ Everglades National Park

Hawaii

☐ Haleakala National Park
☐ Hawai'i Volcanoes National Park

Idaho

☐ Yellowstone National Park

Kentucky

☐ Mammoth Cave National Park

Indiana

☐ Indiana Dunes National Park

Maine

☐ Acadia National Park

Michigan

☐ Isle Royale National Park

Minnesota

☐ Voyageurs National Park

Missouri

☐ Gateway Arch National Park

Montana

☐ Glacier National Park
☐ Yellowstone National Park

Nevada

☐ Death Valley National Park
☐ Great Basin National Park

New Mexico

☐ Carlsbad Caverns National Park
☐ White Sands National Park

North Dakota

☐ Theodore Roosevelt National Park

North Carolina

☐ Great Smoky Mountains National Park

Ohio

☐ Cuyahoga Valley National Park

Oregon

☐ Crater Lake National Park

South Carolina

☐ Congaree National Park

South Dakota

☐ Badlands National Park
☐ Wind Cave National Park

Tennessee

☐ Great Smoky Mountains National Park

Texas

☐ Big Bend National Park
☐ Guadalupe Mountains National Park

Utah

☐ Arches National Park
☐ Bryce Canyon National Park
☐ Canyonlands National Park
☐ Capitol Reef National Park
☐ Zion National Park

Virgin Islands

☐ Virgin Islands National Park

Virginia

☐ Shenandoah National Park

Washington

☐ Mount Rainier National Park
☐ North Cascades National Park
☐ Olympic National Park

West Virginia

☐ New River Gorge National Park

Wyoming

☐ Grand Teton National Park
☐ Yellowstone National Park

Other National Parks

Besides New River Gorge National Park, there are 62 other diverse and beautiful national parks across the United States. Try your hand at this crossword. If you need help, look at the previous page for some hints.

Down

1. State where Acadia National Park is located
2. This national park has the Spanish word for turtle in it.
3. Number of national parks in Alaska
5. This national park has some of the hottest temperatures in the world.
6. This national park is the only one in Idaho.
7. This toothsome creature can be famously found in Everglades National Park.
8. Only president with a national park named for them

Across

4. This state has the most national parks.
9. This park has some of the newest land in the US, caused by volcanic eruptions.
10. This park has the deepest lake in the United States.
11. This color shows up in the name of a national park in California.
12. This national park deserves a gold medal.

Which National Park Will You Go to Next? Word Search

1. Zion
2. Big Bend
3. Glacier
4. Olympic
5. Sequoia
6. Bryce
7. Mesa Verde
8. Biscayne
9. Wind Cave
10. Great Basin
11. Katmai
12. Yellowstone
13. Voyageurs
14. Arches
15. Badlands
16. Denali
17. Glacier Bay
18. Hot Springs

F	M	M	E	S	A	V	E	R	D	E	B	N	E	Y
E	A	B	I	G	B	E	N	D	E	S	A	S	E	M
Y	L	I	C	A	L	O	Y	N	E	E	D	L	T	G
D	M	G	A	S	S	A	U	C	N	R	L	U	E	R
C	E	L	I	I	T	S	C	R	E	O	A	A	K	E
S	N	A	W	Y	E	E	O	I	W	T	N	A	C	A
G	I	C	H	A	A	Q	C	S	E	M	D	N	S	T
N	O	I	Z	P	R	U	T	I	M	R	S	N	E	B
I	W	E	L	M	P	O	N	B	W	E	B	K	H	A
R	J	R	F	D	N	I	F	L	I	H	B	U	C	S
P	A	B	E	E	S	A	N	E	S	O	P	W	R	I
S	J	A	E	N	Y	A	C	S	I	B	A	U	A	N
T	C	Y	I	A	D	O	H	H	Y	M	E	A	L	R
O	T	A	T	L	M	L	E	S	E	G	R	W	R	J
H	S	T	O	I	K	A	T	M	A	I	R	O	P	B
I	C	H	U	R	C	O	L	Y	M	P	I	C	O	U
O	Y	G	T	S	D	E	O	S	B	R	Y	C	E	T
W	I	N	D	C	A	V	E	I	N	R	O	H	E	M

Field Notes

Spend some time to reflect on your trip to New River Gorge National Park. Your field notes will help you remember the things you experienced. Use the space below to write about your day.

While I was at New River Gorge National Park...

I saw:

I heard:

I felt:

Draw a picture of your favorite thing in the park.

I wondered:

ANSWER KEY

National Park Emblem Answers

1. This represents all plants. **Sequoia Tree**
2. This represents all animals. **Bison**
3. This symbol represents the landscapes. **Mountains**
4. This represents the waters protected by the park service. **Water**
5. This represents the historical and archeological values. **Arrowhead**

Jumbles Answers

1. BOATING
2. HIKING
3. BIRDING
4. CAMPING
5. PICNICKING
6. SIGHTSEEING
7. SNOWSHOEING

Go Birdwatching on the Kaymoor Miner's Trail

start
here

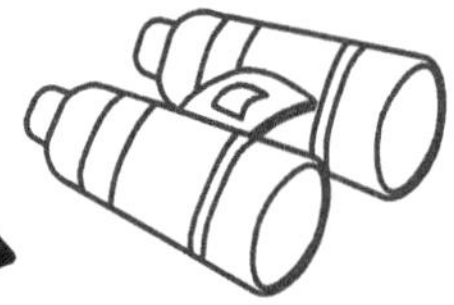

Answers: Who lives here?

Here are eight plants and animals that live in the park.
Use the word bank to fill in the clues below.

WORD BANK: GARTER SNAKE, HAWK, PEREGRINE, HELLBENDER, INDIANA BAT, GROUNDHOG, BLACK BEAR, BEAVER

GROU **N** DHOG

BLACK B **E** AR

HA **W** K

PEREG **R** INE

IND **I** ANA BAT

BEA **V** ER

HELLB **E** NDER

GARTE **R** SNAKE

Find the Match!
Common Names and Latin Names

Match the common name to the scientific name for each animal. The first one is done for you. Use clues on the page before and after this one to complete the matches.

North American Beaver	Haliaeetus leucocephalus
Big Rhododendron	Ursus americanus
White Oak	Crytobranchus alleganiensis
American Black Bear	Falco peregrinus
Great Horned Owl	Rhododendron maximum
Bald Eagle	Thamnophis sirtalis sirtalis
Hellbender	Bubo virginianus
Peregrine Falcon	Castor canadensis
Eastern Garter Snake	Quercus alba

Bald Eagle

Haliaeetus leucocephalus

Answers: The Ten Essentials

The ten essentials is a list of things that are important to have when you go for longer hikes. If you go on a hike to the backcountry, it is especially important that you have everything you need in case of an emergency. If you get lost or something unforeseen happens, it is good to be prepared to survive until help finds you.

The ten essentials list was developed in the 1930s by an outdoors group called the Mountaineers. Over time and technological advancements, this list has evolved. Can you identify all the things on the current list? Circle each of the "essentials" and cross out everything that doesn't make the cut.

fire: matches, lighter, tinder and/or stove	a pint of milk	extra money	headlamp plus extra batteries	extra clothes
extra water	a dog	Polaroid camera	bug net	lightweight game like a deck of cards
extra food	a roll of duct tape	shelter	sun protection like sunglasses, sun-protective clothes and sunscreen	knife: plus a gear repair kit
a mirror	navigation: map, compass, altimeter, GPS device, or satellite messenger	first aid kit	extra flip-flops	entertainment like video games or books

Backcountry- a remote undeveloped rural area.

New River Gorge Word Search

Words may be horizontal, vertical, or diagonal
and they might be backward!

1. West Virginia
2. river
3. rafting
4. wildflowers
5. whitewater
6. coal
7. peregrine
8. fishing
9. climbing
10. Thurmond
11. railroad
12. deer
13. bridge
14. Grandview
15. Sandstone Falls
16. Endless Wall
17. bat
18. woodrat

S	M	R	E	W	I	L	D	F	L	O	W	E	R	S
R	A	F	T	I	N	G	T	O	R	B	R	N	A	W
I	W	N	O	E	P	C	L	I	M	B	I	N	G	H
V	C	H	D	E	E	R	C	L	T	C	B	U	H	I
E	A	F	A	S	E	S	T	E	S	A	P	W	A	T
R	J	I	S	L	T	H	U	R	M	O	N	D	I	E
P	O	S	O	V	E	O	S	B	H	T	A	S	N	W
E	L	H	A	G	R	A	N	D	V	I	E	W	I	A
R	T	I	T	M	D	L	A	E	R	E	L	W	G	T
E	S	N	U	L	E	E	R	T	F	N	A	O	R	E
G	G	G	R	F	W	O	O	D	R	A	T	S	I	R
R	N	B	A	T	F	R	G	R	K	H	L	A	V	A
I	I	E	I	I	A	I	O	I	C	O	A	L	T	N
N	P	B	L	R	S	C	N	N	A	M	C	N	S	P
E	M	N	R	E	R	I	D	B	R	I	D	G	E	O
I	K	A	O	A	K	I	N	G	E	R	A	Q	W	N
O	C	R	A	G	D	E	E	O	O	O	R	V	W	D
N	E	N	D	L	E	S	S	W	A	L	L	A	D	M

Answers: Find the Match!

What are Baby Animals Called?

Match the animal to its baby. The first one is done for you.

Elk	eaglet
Bald Eagle	calf
Little Brown Bat	snakelets
Striped Skunk	pup
Great Horned Owl	owlet
Western Toad	kit
Mountain Lion	tadpole
Garter snake	kitten

Solution: Hike to a Waterfall

DID YOU KNOW?

You can visit many different waterfalls at New River Gorge National Park.

Rockclimbing Route Names

A climbing route is a specific path for climbing up a rock wall. Different features provide handhold and footholds to get climbers to the top. Rock climbers have a reputation for naming their routes quirky names. Find these route names in the word search below.

1. Barb Wire
2. Burning Calves
3. Chewy
4. Chuckles
5. Fantasy
6. Fishbone
7. Floaters
8. Jaws
9. New Yosemite
10. Ritz Cracker
11. Smore Energy
12. Spiderwalk
13. Super Crack
14. Supermoon
15. Werewolf
16. Wild seed
17. Zag
18. Barfing Butterflies

B	B	N	E	W	Y	O	S	E	M	I	T	E	R	S
Z	A	G	T	I	C	H	U	C	K	L	E	S	A	W
I	R	R	O	E	P	C	P	I	M	B	I	P	G	H
V	F	F	L	O	A	T	E	R	S	C	B	I	H	I
E	I	B	A	I	E	S	R	E	S	A	P	D	A	T
R	N	I	U	L	N	H	M	R	J	C	H	E	W	Y
P	G	S	O	R	E	G	O	B	H	T	A	R	N	W
W	B	H	A	G	N	A	O	D	V	J	A	W	S	A
I	U	R	N	M	D	I	N	F	A	N	T	A	S	Y
L	T	N	U	L	E	E	N	T	T	N	A	L	R	F
D	T	G	R	F	W	O	O	G	R	T	T	K	I	I
S	E	B	A	S	U	P	E	R	C	R	A	C	K	S
E	R	I	W	B	R	A	B	I	C	A	A	R	T	H
E	F	I	S	H	B	O	N	E	A	M	L	N	S	P
D	L	N	R	E	R	I	D	B	R	I	D	V	E	O
R	I	T	Z	C	R	A	C	K	E	R	A	Q	E	N
O	E	R	A	G	D	F	L	O	W	E	R	E	W	S
N	S	M	O	R	E	E	N	E	R	G	Y	A	D	M

Answers: Leave No Trace Quiz

Leave No Trace is a concept that helps people make decisions during outdoor recreation that protects the environment. There are seven principles that guide us when we spend time outdoors, whether you are in a national park or not. Are you an expert in Leave No Trace? Take this quiz and find out!

1. How can you plan ahead and prepare to ensure you have the best experience you can in the National Park?
   A. Make sure you stop by the ranger station for a map and to ask about current conditions.
2. What is an example of traveling on a durable surface?
   A. Walking only on the designated path.
3. Why should you dispose of waste properly?
   C. So that other peoples' experiences of the park are not impacted by you leaving your waste behind.
4. How can you best follow the concept "leave what you find"?
   B. Take pictures but leave any physical items where they are.
5. What is not a good example of minimizing campfire impacts?
   C. Building a new campfire ring in a location that has a better view.
6. What is a poor example of respecting wildlife?
   A. Building squirrel houses out of rocks from the river so the squirrels have a place to live.
7. How can you show consideration of other visitors?
   B. Wear headphones on the trail if you choose to listen to music.

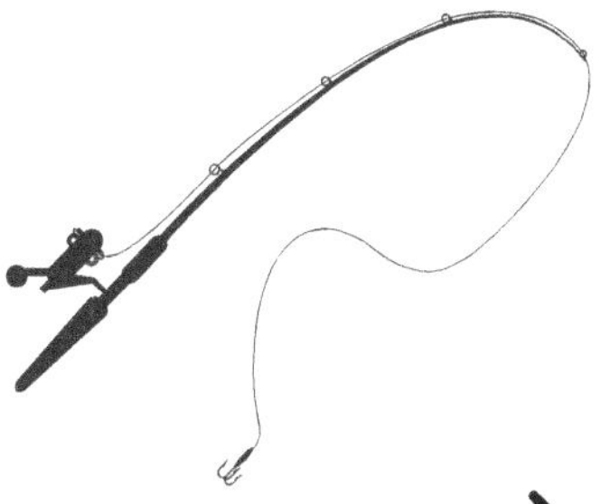

Solution: Catch a Fish in the New River

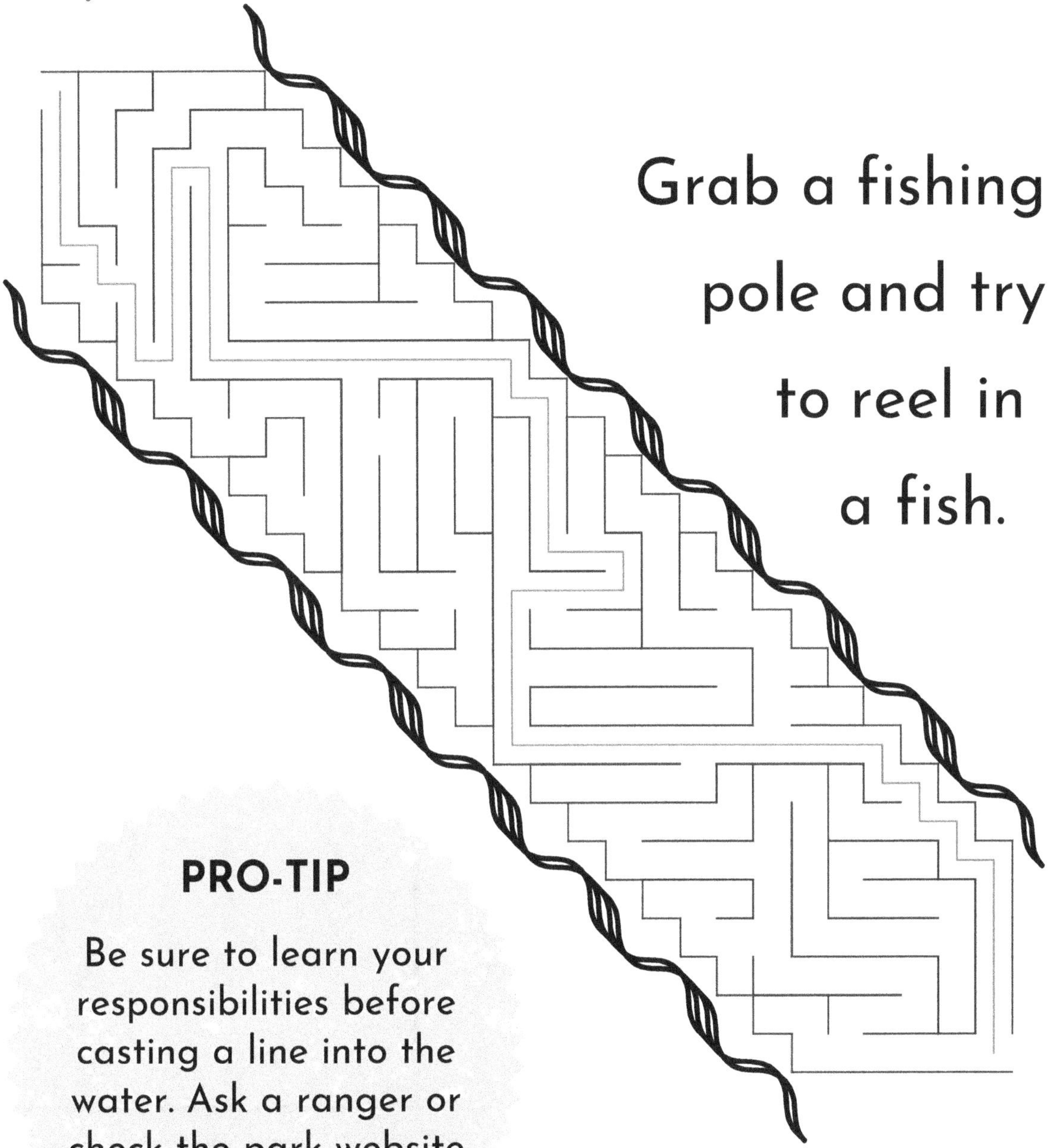

Grab a fishing pole and try to reel in a fish.

PRO-TIP

Be sure to learn your responsibilities before casting a line into the water. Ask a ranger or check the park website before you go.

Decoding Using American Sign Language

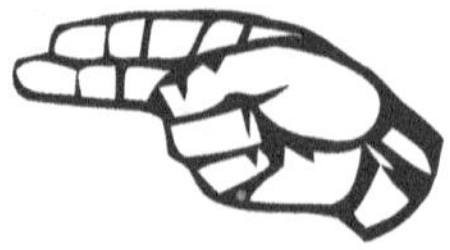

American Sign Language, also called ASL for short, is a language that many people who are deaf or hard of hearing use to communicate. People use ASL to communicate with their hands. Did you know people from all over the country and world travel to national parks? You may hear people speaking other languages. You might also see people using ASL. Use the American Manual Alphabet chart to decode some national parks facts.

This was the first national park to be established:

Y E L L O W S T O N E

This is the biggest national park in the US:

W R A N G E L L -

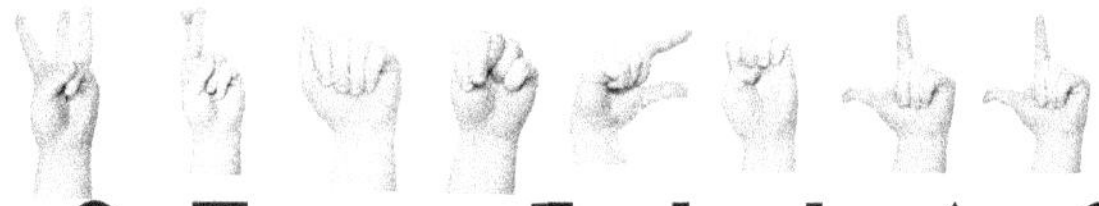

S T . E L I A S

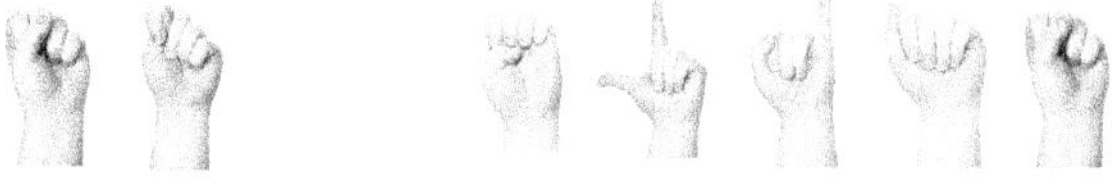

This is the most visited national park:

G R E A T S M O K Y

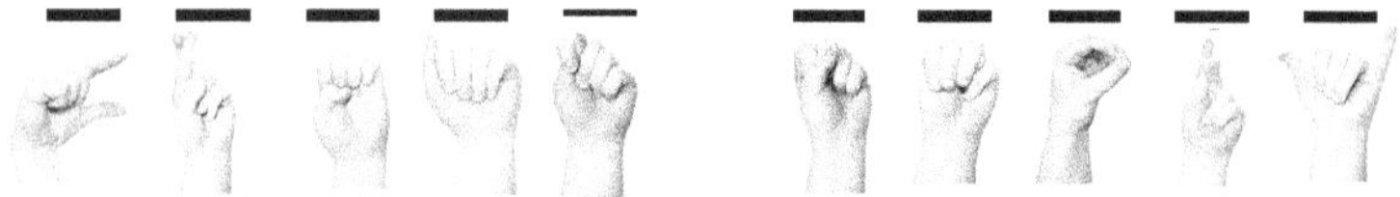

M O U N T A I N S

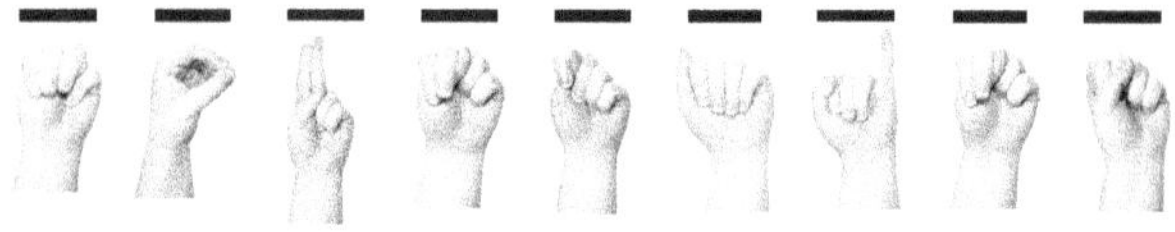

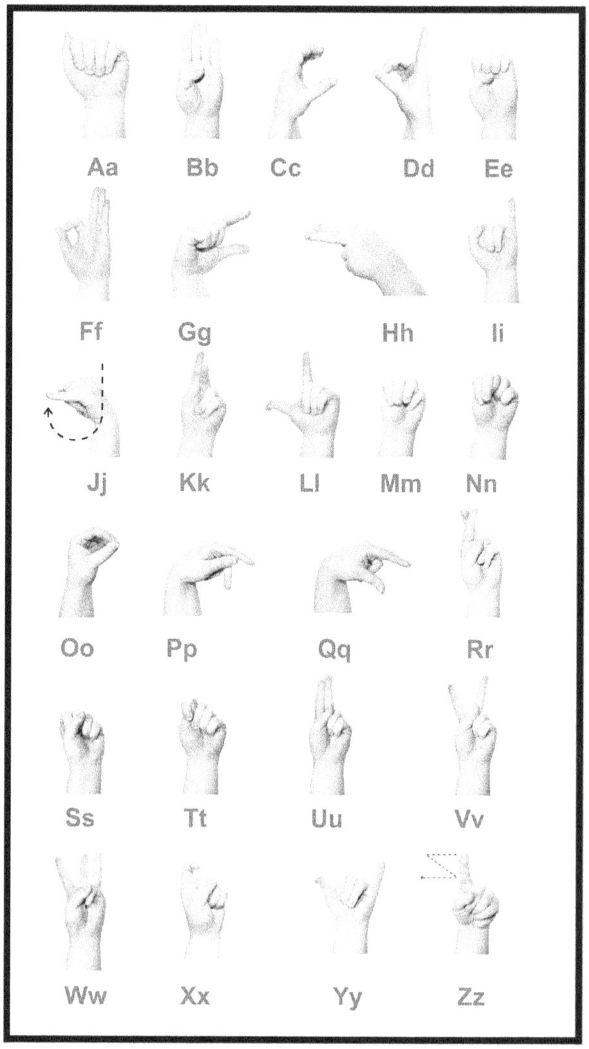

Hint: Pay close attention to the position of the thumb!

Try it! Using the chart, try to make the letters of the alphabet with your hand. What is the hardest letter to make? Can you spell out your name? Show a friend or family member and have them watch you spell out the name of the national park you are in.

Go Bicycling on the Arrowhead Trails

start here

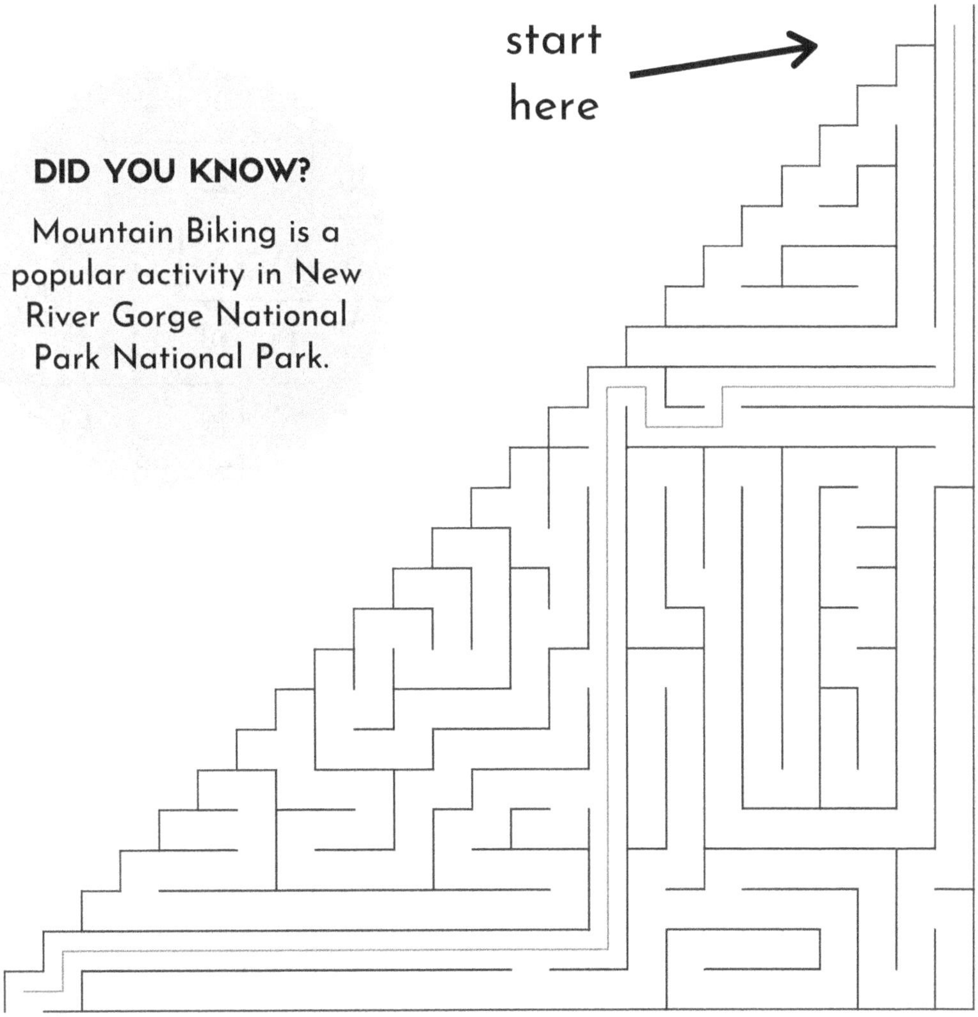

DID YOU KNOW?

Mountain Biking is a popular activity in New River Gorge National Park National Park.

Don't forget to wear a helmet!

Let's Go Camping Word Search

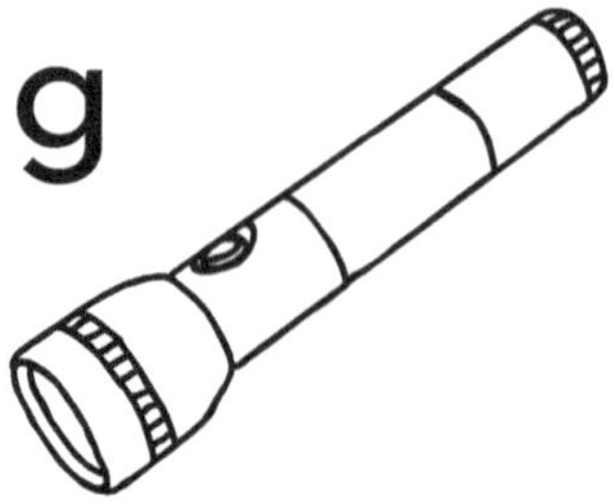

1. tent
2. camp stove
3. sleeping bag
4. bug spray
5. sunscreen
6. map
7. flashlight
8. pillow
9. lantern
10. ice
11. snacks
12. smores
13. water
14. first aid kit
15. chair
16. cards
17. books
18. games
19. trail
20. hat

D	P	P	I	L	L	O	W	D	B	T	E	A	C	I
E	O	A	D	P	R	E	A	A	M	B	R	C	A	N
P	W	C	A	M	P	S	T	O	V	E	I	H	X	G
R	A	H	S	G	E	L	E	B	E	E	D	A	P	S
E	L	B	U	G	S	P	R	A	Y	N	G	I	E	A
S	I	A	H	G	C	I	C	N	N	M	E	R	C	N
C	W	N	L	A	F	I	R	S	K	O	O	B	F	K
M	T	A	E	M	I	L	E	L	H	M	R	W	L	J
T	A	P	R	E	A	O	R	E	S	L	B	A	A	B
S	M	P	A	S	R	R	T	E	N	T	L	U	S	C
C	E	A	I	I	R	C	G	P	E	I	U	J	H	A
S	S	N	A	C	K	S	S	I	M	O	K	I	L	R
I	J	R	S	F	O	I	S	N	J	R	A	Q	I	D
C	Y	E	T	L	E	V	E	G	U	O	R	V	G	S
E	W	T	A	K	C	A	B	B	S	S	O	H	H	M
X	J	N	F	I	R	S	T	A	I	D	K	I	T	T
U	A	A	E	S	S	E	N	G	E	T	P	V	A	B
C	J	L	I	A	R	T	D	N	A	M	A	H	A	S

Fish of the New River

1.

2.

Unscramble these common fish names that live in the park.

3.

4.

5.

1. WALLEYE
2. TROUT
3. BLUEGILL
4. CATFISH
5. BASS

Word Bank

- bluegill
- trout
- carp
- minnow
- crappie
- bass
- walleye
- catfish

Answers: Other National Parks

Down

1. State where Acadia National Park is located
2. This National Park has the Spanish word for turtle in it
3. Number of National Parks in Alaska
5. This National Park has some of the hottest temperatures in the world
6. This National Park is the only one in Idaho
7. This toothsome creature can be famously found in Everglades National Park
8. Only president with a national park named for them

Across

4.This state has the most National Parks
9.This park has some of the newest land in the US, caused by a volcanic eruption
10. This park has the deepest lake in the United States
11. This color shows up in the name of a National Park in California
12.This National Park deserves a gold medal

Answers: Where National Park Will You Go Next?

1. Zion
2. Big Bend
3. Glacier
4. Olympic
5. Sequoia
6. Bryce
7. Mesa Verde
8. Biscayne
9. Wind Cave
10. Great Basin
11. Katmai
12. Yellowstone
13. Voyageurs
14. Arches
15. Badlands
16. Denali
17. Glacier Bay
18. Hot Springs

F	M	M	E	S	A	V	E	R	D	E	B	N	E	Y
E	A	B	I	G	B	E	N	D	E	S	A	S	E	M
Y	L	I	C	A	L	O	Y	N	E	E	D	L	T	G
D	M	G	A	S	S	A	U	C	N	R	L	U	E	R
C	E	L	I	I	T	S	C	R	E	O	A	A	K	E
S	N	A	W	Y	E	E	O	I	W	T	N	A	C	A
G	I	C	H	A	A	Q	C	S	E	M	D	N	S	T
N	O	I	Z	P	R	U	T	I	M	R	S	N	E	B
I	W	E	L	M	P	O	N	B	W	E	B	K	H	A
R	J	R	F	D	N	I	F	L	I	H	B	U	C	S
P	A	B	E	E	S	A	N	E	S	O	P	W	R	I
S	J	A	E	N	Y	A	C	S	I	B	A	U	A	N
T	C	Y	I	A	D	O	H	H	Y	M	E	A	L	R
O	T	A	T	L	M	L	E	S	E	G	R	W	R	J
H	S	T	O	I	K	A	T	M	A	I	R	O	P	B
I	C	H	U	R	C	O	L	Y	M	P	I	C	O	U
O	Y	G	T	S	D	E	O	S	B	R	Y	C	E	T
W	I	N	D	C	A	V	E	I	N	R	O	H	E	M

LITTLE BISON

Press

Little Bison Press is an independent children's book publisher based in the Pacific Northwest. We promote exploration, conservation, and adventure through our books. Established in 2021, our passion for outside spaces and travel inspired the creation of Little Bison Press.

We seek to publish books that support children in learning about and caring for the natural places in our world.

To learn more, visit:

LittleBisonPress.com

www.ingramcontent.com/pod-product-compliance
Lightning Source LLC
Chambersburg PA
CBHW081349070526
44578CB00005B/779
9781956614077